T0393599

MEET THE ROYALS

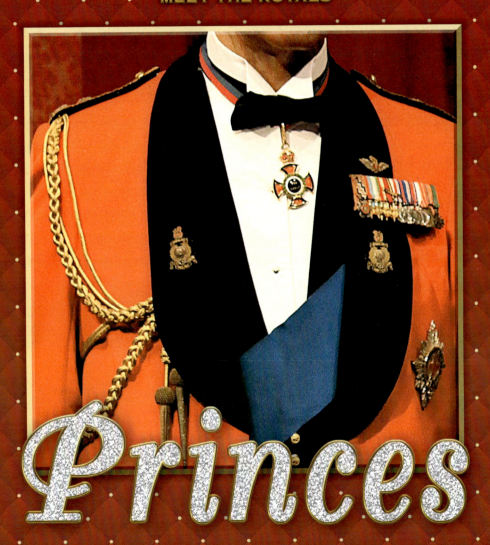

Princes

Enslow Publishing
101 W. 23rd Street
Suite 240
New York, NY 10011
USA

enslow.com

Sarita McDaniel

WORDS TO KNOW

custom A habit or tradition of a group of people.

inherit To pass from parent to child.

military The group of soldiers that protects and serves an area.

monarchy A country ruled by a king or queen.

princess The daughter of a king or queen.

represent To stand for; to be a symbol of something.

royalty A person who is related to the king or queen.

throne The place where a king or queen sits, or the monarch's role as leader.

CONTENTS

WORDS TO KNOW 2

THE ROYAL FAMILY 5

SOME WILL BE KING 7

WHO CAN RULE? 9

SCHOOLWORK 11

KNIGHTS 13

SOLDIER PRINCE 15

ATTENDING EVENTS 17

FINDING A WIFE 19

FREE TO CHOOSE 21

A SYMBOL OF THE COUNTRY 23

LEARN MORE 24

INDEX 24

Britain's Queen Elizabeth II married Prince Philip in 1947. Their children include Prince Charles (right) and Princess Anne.

The Royal Family

Some countries are ruled by a king or queen. This is called a **monarchy**. The king or queen may have brothers, sisters, sons, and daughters. They are all part of the royal family.

Fast Fact
Today there are 44 countries that have kings or queens.

The Crown Prince and Crown Princess of Norway will rule the country one day.

Some Will Be King

A prince is the son of a king or queen. Some princes will be kings when they grow up. Some princes will not. It's commonly the oldest son who **inherits** the **throne**.

Fast Fact
The person next in line to inherit the throne is called an heir.

Naruhito, Crown Prince of Japan, stands with his wife on their wedding day.

WHO CAN RULE?

In some countries, only princes can become the ruler. In other countries, the oldest child inherits the throne. It can be a prince or **princess**.

Fast Fact

Kings rule until they die or decide to give up the throne.

Britain's Prince George heads off to his first day of nursery school.

SCHOOLWORK

Princes have to be good students. They work hard at school to learn how to run their country.

Fast Fact
Prince Naruhito of Japan studied at Oxford University.

Many years ago, princes often became knights.

KNIGHTS

A long time ago, many princes trained to be knights. They rode horses and fought in battles. Today, many princes choose to join the **military**. They want to serve their country.

Fast Fact

Britain's Prince Harry was knighted in 2015.

Princes William and Harry wore their military uniforms at Harry's wedding.

Soldier Prince

Prince William and Prince Harry both served in the British Army and the Royal Air Force. Prince Haakon of Norway served in his country's Royal Navy.

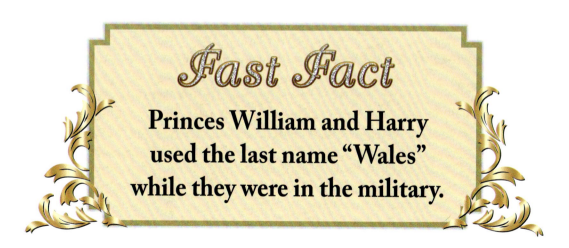

Fast Fact
Princes William and Harry used the last name "Wales" while they were in the military.

Prince Moulay El Hassan of Morocco stands between his father, the king, and the French president.

Attending Events

As princes grow up, they have more royal jobs. They go to important events with their parents. They meet with people from their country. They learn what it would be like to be king.

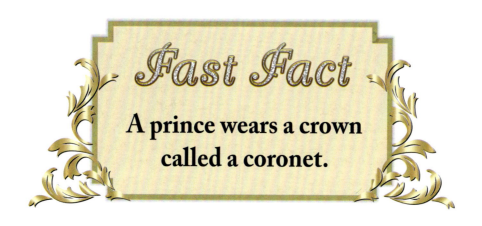

Fast Fact

A prince wears a crown called a coronet.

King Edward VII of the United Kingdom and his wife Alexandra were matched up by Queen Victoria.

Finding a Wife

In the past, the king or queen chose a wife for the prince. A prince from one country married a princess from another country. This helped the two countries stay friendly.

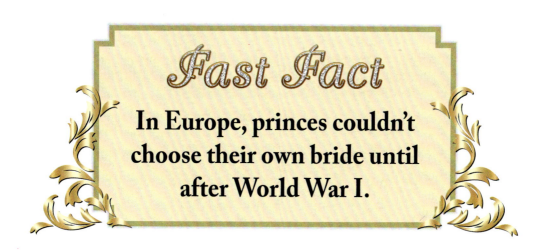

Fast Fact

In Europe, princes couldn't choose their own bride until after World War I.

Prince William married Kate Middleton in 2011. He is next in line to become king after his father, Prince Charles.

Free to Choose

Today, most princes are free to marry anyone they choose. A prince can even marry someone who is not a member of the **royalty**.

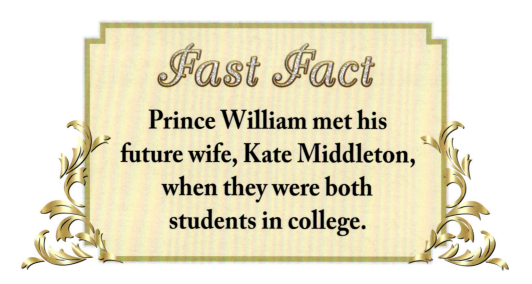

Fast Fact

Prince William met his future wife, Kate Middleton, when they were both students in college.

Prince Charles met with American president Barack Obama at the White House in 2011.

A Symbol of the Country

A prince **represents** the royal family wherever he goes. He must learn about the **customs** of countries he visits. A prince must show respect for everyone he meets.

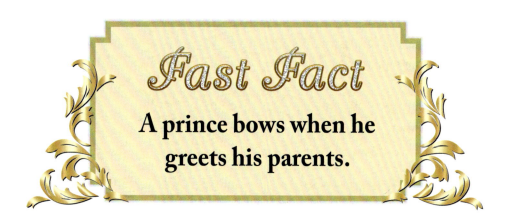

Fast Fact
A prince bows when he greets his parents.

LEARN MORE

BOOKS

DK. *Castles*. New York, NY: DK, 2019.

Gagne, Tammy. *Prince Harry*. Hallandale, FL: Mitchell Lane, 2018.

Howell, Izzi. *Prince Charles*. Sydney, Australia: Hachette, 2019.

WEBSITES

The Home of the Royal Family
royal.uk
Find out more about the British royal family.

DK Find Out Kings and Queens
dkfindout.com/us/history/kings-and-queens/
Learn more about monarchs throughout history.

INDEX

Britain, 4, 10, 13, 15
crown prince, 6, 8
heir, 7
king, 5, 7, 9, 16, 17, 19

Prince Charles, 4, 20, 22
Prince George, 10

Prince Harry, 13, 14, 15
Prince William, 14, 15, 20, 21

princess, 9, 19
queen, 5, 7, 19
royal family, 5, wife, 19, 21

Published in 2020 by Enslow Publishing, LLC
101 W. 23rd Street, Suite 240, New York, NY 10011
Copyright © 2020 by Enslow Publishing, LLC
All rights reserved.
No part of this book may be reproduced by any means without the written permission of the publisher.

Library of Congress Cataloging-in-Publication Data
Names: McDaniel, Sarita, author.
Title: Princes / Sarita McDaniel.
Description: New York : Enslow Publishing, 2020 | Series: Meet the royals | Includes bibliographical references and index. | Audience: Grades K–3.
Identifiers: LCCN 2019010894| ISBN 9781978511873 (library bound) | ISBN 9781978511859 (pbk.) | ISBN 9781978511866 (6 pack)
Subjects: LCSH: Princes—Juvenile literature.
Classification: LCC D412.7 .M38 2019 | DDC 305.5/22—dc23
LC record available at https://lccn.loc.gov/2019010894

Printed in the United States of America

To Our Readers: We have done our best to make sure website addresses in this book were active and appropri when we went to press. However, the author and the publis have no control over and assume no liability for the mate available on those websites or on any websites they may to. Any comments or suggestions can be sent by e-mai customerservice@enslow.com.

Photo Credits: Cover, p. 1 Lorna Roberts/Shutterstock.c p. 4 Lisa Sheridan/Hulton Royals Collection/Getty Ima p. 6 Patrick van Katwijk/Getty Images; p. 8 Toshifumi Kitam AFP/Getty Images; p. 10 Getty Images; p. 12 North W Picture Archives/Alamy Stock Photo ; p. 14 Max Mun Indigo/Getty Images; p. 16 Chesnot/Getty Images; p Universal History Archive/Universal Images Group/G Images; p. 20 Sean Gallup/Getty Images; p. 22 Alex W Getty Images; cover, p. 1 (background), interior pages (bord Alona Syplyak/Shutterstock.com, cover and interior p (decorative motifs) View Pixel/Shutterstock.com.